Making
Birdhouses

Making
Birdhouses

ANDREW NEWTON-COX
AND DEENA BEVERLEY

LORENZ BOOKS
NEW YORK • LONDON • SYDNEY • BATH

Dedicated to Jane Wilson

First published in 1997 by Lorenz Books

Paperback edition published in 1998 by Lorenz Books
an imprint of Anness Publishing Inc., 27 West 20th Street, New York, NY 10011

Loren Books are available for bulk purchase for sales promotion and
for premium use. For details, write or call the sales director,
Lorenz Books, 27 West 20th Street, New York, NY 10011;
(800) 354-9657

© 1997 Anness Publishing Limited

ISBN 1 85967 673 1

Publisher: Joanna Lorenz
Senior Editor: Lindsay Porter
Designer: Caroline Reeves
Photographer: David Parmiter
Stylist: Deena Beverley
Illustrators: Lucinda Ganderton and Vana Haggerty

Publisher's Note:
Craft and woodworking projects are very rewarding, but when using any tools or equipment be careful
and wear the proper protective clothing. The authors and publishers have made every effort to ensure that
the projects in this book are accurate and safe, and cannot accept liability for any damage or injury.

Printed and bound in China

1 3 5 7 9 10 8 6 4 2

Contents

Introduction

Perhaps it is the opportunity to create a world in miniature from almost any available material while simultaneously giving nature a helping hand that has ensured the continued popularity of bird-housing as a thriving folk art around the globe.

Birdhouses can be plain, pretty or whimsical without affecting their primary function. Once the basic size and safety requirements have been satisfied, the finish of the exterior is up to the individual.

The projects in this book are practical and beautiful solutions for providing food, drink and shelter for the feathered community.

Even unoccupied birdhouses make charming decorative features for either an interior or a garden, and collecting antique birdhouses is a growing trend. We do hope that you take this opportunity to create your own heirloom piece.

From rudimentary woodwork to more complex mixed media creations, there is something here for every skill level. New skills can be acquired while creating something that will be of lasting benefit and enjoyment to birds and humans alike.

Happy birdhousing!

Providing a Place to Nest

Above: A wicker beehive-style house is ideal for smaller birds, and makes a decorative addition to the garden.

Even in an urban garden, birds will find many nooks and crannies for nesting. Just a little encouragement in the form of providing suitable nest boxes will ensure that birds breed, as well as feed, in your garden.

Nest boxes

An excellent way to follow birds' progress in your garden is to install a nest box. In addition to the many designs and ideas provided in this book, specialty organizations will give good advice on building rudimentary but effective boxes, along with detailed advice about different species and their preferences.

Choosing a site

There may be natural possibilities already in your garden that, with a little thought, can be turned into good nest sites. Birds may nest in an old shed with the door left purposely ajar, or make their homes in a hole in the eaves of a house or shed. Thick hedges, rotten trees, unclipped bramble bushes and log piles are all potential homes. Place any box away from possible disturbances, approximately 6½ feet up a wall or tree trunk. Face the box away from prevailing wind and rain, and do not position it to face south, as the sun will overheat the chicks and eggs. Place open-fronted nest boxes in thick cover.

Avoiding predators

Fledglings must learn to survive, so any human intervention is not a good idea, but you can help by attaching a bell to your cat's collar to at least alert birds to the presence of lurking felines. Prickly, cat-deterring plants around the nest sites may help, along with scents to ward off cats, such as certain commercial products and essential oil sprays. The best cat deterrent is probably a dog.

Other threats include magpies, which attack the open nests of birds such as finches and blackbirds. Great spotted woodpeckers, which can hack their way through the side of a nest box, can be deterred by incorporating metal plates in the box.

Although it may seem cruel, should you find a fledgling or nestling on the ground, leave it alone and let nature take its course. Remember that nature is about survival of the fittest.

Right: Robins, among other species of bird, enjoy open-fronted boxes.

INSTALLING A NEST BOX

There are a few simple rules to consider when installing a nest box of any type:
• Be patient. It may take several seasons before any birds settle in the boxes. When birds do settle, do not interfere. Enjoy them from a distance.
• Avoid placing a feeding table near a nesting box. The nesting birds would suffer greatly from the presence of feeding birds so close to their home.
• Be aware that a perch close to the entrance hole may also assist predatory access.
• Be restrained. One or two boxes in the average garden is enough. Any more than that will cause distress.
• Place the nest box in situ in the autumn so that it will weather (and possibly supply winter roosting) for when the spring breeding season arrives.
• Clean out used nest boxes with plain, boiling water at the end of the season (around November) to kill any lurking parasites.

Above: The long chimney-like shape of this box will attract owls, which tend to nest in hollow trees.

Above: Although customized and embellished, this house still retains its practical elements, providing a perch to allow access to the inside and a small entrance hole to keep out larger birds.

Basic types of nest box

There are several types of nest box, each designed for particular types of bird. For example, smaller titmice need smaller entrance holes than larger titmice, to prevent the larger bird from evicting the smaller one when the inevitable territorial disputes arise.

Robins and other similar birds may make their homes in open-fronted nest boxes. Owls prefer a chimney-like box that mimics the hollow ends of branches in which they naturally nest. This type of box is particularly welcome where a known nest site has been lost because of storm damage. Attach the box at a 45-degree angle on a tree, drill drainage holes in the bottom and add a layer of wood or stone chips inside. Owls are protected by law in some countries, and if this is the case, occupied nests should not be visited without a license – even if you have installed the box yourself. It is a good idea to contact a specialty organization for advice.

Special boxes may also be built for kestrels and woodpeckers. If you are very interested in nature, you will probably want to add homes for hedgehogs and squirrels, too. Wildlife organizations are a great source of up-to-date information.

Attracting Birds

Above: Lard cakes studded with seeds appeal to many varieties of bird.

Right: Roofed bird tables will keep the birds - and food - dry in inclement weather. This one was made from pieces of fallen wood collected from the forest floor.

Below: Be sure to supply a source of water, particularly if you are providing dried food during the winter months.

The simplest way to attract birds to your garden or window box is to put out food for them, particularly during the winter months when natural food becomes scarce. However, you may provide appropriate food throughout the year if you wish.

Whatever feeding method you decide upon, be consistent. A wasted journey to an empty bird table uses a bird's precious energy supply, especially as winter progresses and food becomes more difficult to find. Ideally, feed twice a day in winter: once in the early morning and again in the early afternoon.

In spring and summer, feeding can still be helpful, but do follow these rules for safety and hygiene: do not use peanuts unless they are in a mesh container. This will prevent the larger pieces, which can choke baby birds, from being removed. In summer, avoid fat cakes; the fat will melt and become very messy, and can also glue birds' beaks together.

Above: The wire mesh around the food source keeps birds from extracting whole peanuts. This is particularly important during the nesting season, because young nestlings and fledglings can choke on whole nuts.

Where to feed

Ideally, a bird table should be placed approximately 6–10 feet from a bush or tree, where the birds can flee in case of danger, and at least 17 feet from a house. Many birds are scared of open sites, but they can have accidents flying into house windows, and may be scared away by the movement of people inside the house. Window stickers featuring birds of prey are available which, when stuck to the window panes, indicate the presence of an otherwise invisible surface and deter smaller birds from flying too close to the house.

Bird tables

A bird table gives you a clear view of feeding birds, and offers them some protection against predators and the elements. If you are making your own table use wood that has not been treated with wood preservative. A roof will keep the food and the birds dry. If you don't make a roof, drill a few holes in the floor of the table for drainage. A small lip around the edge of the food table can prevent lighter foods from being blown away by wind. A bird table must be cleaned occasionally and any food that is past its prime should be removed. An adequate supply of fresh water should be provided year round. It can be as simple as a bowl of water on the surface of the table, or a separate facility.

Below: Seed balls and strings of nuts are a welcome supplement to the meager diet available in winter. Do keep a supply of fresh water on hand as well, as dried food does not contain enough natural moisture.

Above: Hanging feeders offer a pleasant challenge to many species.

Feeding from ground stations

Some birds, such as song thrushes, are habitual ground feeders. Pheasants, finches and mourning doves may also be attracted to ground stations. Place ground stations away from the bird table, if you have one, so the food is not contaminated by droppings from the birds above.

Hanging feeders

Some species, such as titmice, which have adapted to feeding in trees, will benefit from a more challenging feeder. Blue and tufted titmice can cling upside down from various types of hanging feeders, and may be joined by nuthatches. Many types of feeder are available, or you can make or adapt your own. Some foods are also suitable for hanging without a feeder, such as peanuts in shells, half coconuts, popcorn garlands and fat cakes on strings.

What to Feed Birds

Left: A wreath of sliced, glazed cranberries is much appreciated by the feathered community.

Live food
Live food, such as waxworms and mealworms, provides a high-quality source of protein, and encourages a wide variety of species into the garden. Live food is especially useful during harsh weather and can be obtained from suppliers.

Seeds and grains
Use high-quality fresh seeds from a reliable source, not old or stale seeds, as these are neither of interest nor nutritional value to the birds. Sunflower seeds are a good choice, and black sunflower seeds, rather than the striped variety, are the favored food of many species. The skins are the thinnest of all sunflower varieties, making them easy for the birds to open. All types of sunflower seeds are safe for young birds to eat, so they may be offered all year round. Canary seeds, melon seeds, hemp seeds, small wheat, ground and flaked corn, corn kernels and oatmeal are all good sources of nutrition. The mix of seeds may be fine-tuned to attract particular species to your garden. Consult a catalog for more details.

Aside from kitchen scraps, there are many types of food suitable for the birds in your garden. A glance at any birding catalog will reveal dozens of foods designed to attract particular birds. Here are just a few ideas.

Fat products
The best types of base for lard cakes are lamb and beef fats, either in natural form or as processed suet. Because these are hard, they do not melt easily in warm weather and are unlikely to glue birds' beaks together. Manufacturers add supplements to their lard cakes, but you can easily make your own at home with a mixture of seeds, fruits and nuts following the recipe on the next page.

Unsalted peanuts
Buy only high-quality "safe nuts," available at pet stores and certain wildlife sanctuaries, to ensure that the nuts are free from lethal toxins. Make sure that it is difficult to pull a whole, shelled peanut from a feeder, as adult birds have been known to feed these to their young, resulting in fatal choking.

Bird Treats

SUITABILITY OF GENERAL FOODS

Trial and error will prove what goes over best with your feathered population, but here are a few general pointers:

• *Bread* is eaten by many species. Brown is best, but whatever type you offer, make sure that it has been thoroughly soaked in water to prevent it from expanding in the birds' stomachs.
• *Dried fruit* is popular, but should be soaked as for bread.
• *Fresh fruits*, especially pears and apples, are enjoyed by chickadees and thrushes. It is good for the birds to offer these fruits in winter.
• *Grated cheese* is popular, especially with robins.
• *Grit, sand and gravel*, although not actually foodstuffs, aid digestion, especially for seed eaters.
• *Hazelnuts* wedged into tree bark will appeal to nuthatches, which will enjoy hammering them open.
• *Household foods* such as hard-cooked eggs, baked potatoes, uncooked pastry and stale cake and cookies are all widely available choices that birds will enjoy. Feel free to experiment, and be sure not to offer dehydrated or very salty foods, as these can be dangerous.

All of the following recipes are guaranteed to bring flocks of birds to your garden and ensure a happy and satisfied bird community.

Bejeweled apple
An apple stuffed with colorful, nutritious goodies is a visual as well as nourishing feast. Hollow out an apple that is past its prime. Fill it with a mixture of cooked rice, seeds, and rehydrated dried fruit and berries. Make sure the fruit has been thoroughly rehydrated before adding it to the mixture.

Berry, Seed and Golden Kernel Heart
This delectably pretty treat is very easy to make. In a double boiler, melt down some lard. Add rehydrated berries, seeds, nuts and corn kernels. Pour into a heart-shaped pan (the size sold for making single-serving cœur à la crème is perfect). Drape a length of natural garden string into the mixture so that it will emerge from the top of the heart for hanging. Weigh the string down with more fruit and nuts if it rises to the surface. Allow to set thoroughly before removing from the pan. Invert the pan and run a little warm water over it to aid release.

Cranberry Terrine
This is made in a similar way to the Berry, Seed and Golden Kernel Heart. Place a layer of rehydrated cranberries into the base of a single-serving oval pan. Slowly pour in just enough melted lard to secure the berries. Allow to cool and set. When set, add more melted lard to form another layer. Let cool and set before adding the final layer of berries, secured with a little melted lard. Let set, and remove as for the Berry, Seed and Golden Kernel Heart.

Nuts and Berries Festive Loaf
Soak brown bread crumbs in water until soft. Mix in assorted rehydrated berries, seeds and nuts. Grease a single-serving loaf tin, and add the mixture, pressing down well. Bake in a medium oven for approximately 15 minutes or until the top is golden brown and the loaf leaves the sides of the pan. Let cool slightly, remove from the pan and cool on a wire rack.

Orange Sunrise Treat
Hollow out an orange half, and fill with a mixture of muesli, fruit, nuts and seeds, all fully soaked and rehydrated with water before mixing.

Birdbaths

Above: Running water will appeal to the birds as it enhances your garden.

Above: A traditional stone birdbath is an atmospheric addition to any garden.

Right: This contemporary birdbath is a piece of sculpture in its own right.

Opposite: Pieces of broken china make a wonderful mosaic pattern. The sloping sides provide easy access to the water.

Birds need a constant supply of water, both for bathing and for drinking. It is essential for them to keep their feathers in good condition for insulation during the long and bitter nights of winter. Some birds, such as blue titmice, may drink more in winter because their seasonal diet of dry nuts is not sufficient to hydrate them. Seed eaters also need plenty of drinking water to compensate for the lack of moisture in their diet.

Ponds, of course, provide water all year round for bathing and drinking, and attract many other types of wildlife to your garden. We are not all fortunate enough to have the space or the facilities for ponds or larger water sources, but a birdbath is an attractive option which will brighten your garden while bringing great pleasure to the bird population and yourself.

A birdbath doesn't have to be an elaborate affair. A puddle is the simplest form of all. You could make a more permanent watering hole by scraping out a shallow puddle shape in a flower bed, lining it with plastic and securing the plastic in place with stones. Another simple and unobtrusive option might be an inverted trashcan lid placed securely on bricks.

There are many commercially-available birdbaths which not only serve a useful purpose to the birds, but add points of interest to a garden scheme. Fountains, or any form of dripping water, make ponds and baths even more enticing to birds as well as appealing to human visitors.

Whatever the birdbath, make sure that it has either sloping sides or a ramp if the sides are steep, so that birds can walk easily in and out, and small animals do not become trapped. Do be diligent about keeping the birdbath clean and filled with fresh water, and crack any ice which forms on the surface in the winter.

Daisy House

Summer daisies make a stylish statement for the fashionable nesting pair. Roses or another flower of your choice may be substituted to produce customized garden chic.

· ·

TOOLS AND MATERIALS

- 1/4-inch medium-density fiberboard or exterior-grade plywood
- Pencil
- Ruler
- Saw
- White glue
- Hammer
- Paneling pins
- Coping saw

- Drill
- Keyhole saw
- Bench vise
- Latex paint: white, yellow, green and blue
- Medium and fine paintbrushes
- Glue gun and glue sticks
- Exterior-grade varnish

· ·

1 Mark out the basic house onto 1/4-inch fiberboard following the template at the back of the book. Cut out the pieces, and assemble with white glue and paneling pins. Draw flower, petal and leaf shapes onto the face of the board following the diagram on the next page. Make sure the central hole in the front motif will match the size of the entrance hole.

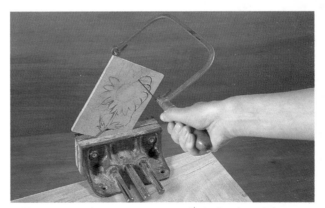

2 Using a coping saw, cut out the leaf and petal shapes. Use a drill and keyhole saw, cut out the central hole of the front motif.. Paint the pieces to represent real daisy colors and let dry. Add details with a fine paintbrush.

• • •➤

17

3 Paint the basic house blue. When dry, embellish with painted grass applied with a fine paintbrush. Paint the entrance hole yellow, but leave the interior unpainted for the health of the birds.

Above: If woodworking is not your forte, this simply painted alternative should appeal. The same basic house is painted in bright colors. A slice cut from a cork forms a jaunty perch which mirrors the loosely applied polka dots.

4 Using a glue gun, stick the shapes permanently to the box. Position the shapes to form a daisy chain across the box, gluing on some fallen petals for added effect. Coat with several layers of exterior-grade varnish.

18

Rustic Feeders

These two feeders in different styles originate from the same basic store-bought model. One has been sanded and painted to resemble driftwood, while the other has been camouflaged beneath found objects ranging from a rusty sheet of tin to plasterer's angle bead. Be creative with the objects you use and give the feeder a flavor of whatever is in its immediate environment, or collect materials while on vacation to produce a delightful memento.

• •

TOOLS AND MATERIALS

• •

- 2 wooden bird feeders
- Light gray latex paint
- Medium paintbrushes
- Sandpaper
- Clear glue
- Sand
- Shells
- Moss
- Stub wires
- Pencil

- Natural twine
- Corks
- Craft knife or scalpel
- Thick florists' wire
- Protective gloves
- Sheet of old tin
- Tin snips or saw
- Glue gun and glue sticks
- Plasterer's angle bead
- Black spray paint

1 Paint the first feeder and allow to dry. Rub down with sandpaper to give the surface a weathered, driftwood effect. Apply clear glue to the roof and sprinkle sand over it. Add seashore finds, such as shells, and moss. Twist lengths of stub wire around a pencil and weave natural twine through them to imitate coils of rope.

2 Use cut-off corks to seal the feed chambers, and tie a loop of florists' wire to suspend the house. • • •▶

19

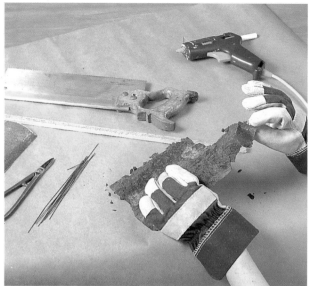

3 For the second feeder, wearing protective gloves, snip pieces of tin to resemble a roof. Remove all sharp edges and glue in place. Glue moss around the base.

Above and right: Two very different results are achieved using the same basic feeder. Experiment with different materials and applications to create your own designs.

4 Make a ridge for the roof from plasterer's angle bead sprayed black. Glue it firmly to the house. Plug the feed holes with corks and suspend with wire as before.

Beach Huts

Build multiples of a basic hut and paint them bright colors to brighten dull days in the garden. With separate residences, territorial disputes should be decided quickly or at least reduced to the simple question of who gets to live at No. 1, The Promenade.

TOOLS AND MATERIALS

- ¹/₂-inch exterior-grade plywood
- Pencil
- Ruler
- Saw
- Compass
- Drill
- Keyhole saw
- Hammer
- Paneling pins
- 6 x 6-inch brass hinge strips
- Screwdriver
- Screws
- ¹/₄-inch exterior-grade plywood
- Coping saw
- Exterior paint: blue, green, pink and white
- Medium paintbrushes

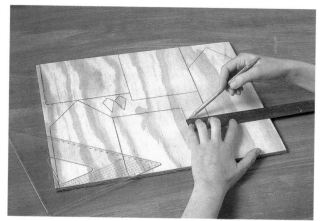

1 Mark the beach hut panels onto the surface of the ¹/₂-inch plywood, following the template at the back of the book. You will need to make six basic beach huts.

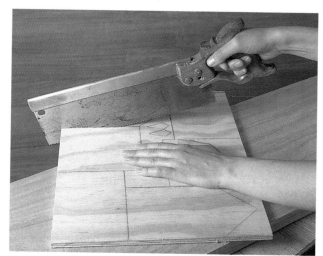

2 Use a saw to cut out each shape. Take care to cut exactly along each pencil line so that the saw cut is divided equally between each panel and the one next to it, to ensure all the pieces are accurate.

3 Mark a vertical line on the front panel. Mark a horizontal line across the panel, at the base of the triangle. Where the two lines cross, draw a 1¹/₄-inch circle using a compass. Cut out the hole by first drilling a pilot hole then enlarging it with a keyhole saw.

5 Attach the brass hinge strip to the edge of the bigger, loose roof piece using a screwdriver and the appropriate size screws.

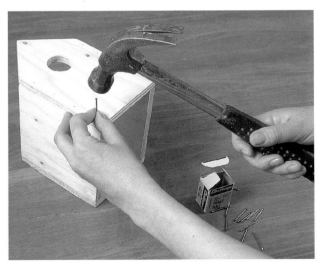

4 Assemble the front, back, sides and the smaller roof piece of the hut using a hammer and paneling pins driven flush with the surface of the wood.

6 Attach the hinged roof half to the hut, making sure the two roof halves overlap the front and rear by the same amount.

•••▶

23

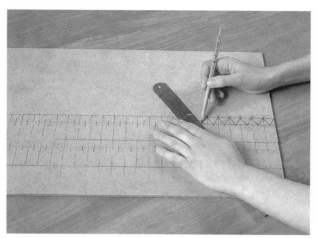

7 Mark out the base and the toothed decorative strips on 1/4-inch board. Mark the teeth by drawing a line 3/4 inch down from the top edge of each 2-inch strip, then ruling off every 3/4 inch along the length. Make a pencil mark halfway between each ruled 3/4-inch section, then join this single mark with the top line at 3/4-inch intervals to form tooth shapes.

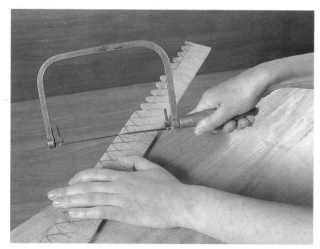

8 Cut the toothing with a coping saw. Fix a toothed decorative strip to each side of the baseboard with paneling pins. Paint with exterior paint, leaving the inside of the huts unpainted for the health of the birds.

Copper Birdbath

You will have hours of pleasure watching the birds preening and cleaning in this beautiful yet eminently practical beaten copper birdbath. Maintain a constant supply of fresh drinking water all year round to ensure the health and happiness of the bird population in your locality.

TOOLS AND MATERIALS

- China marker
- String
- 0.9mm copper sheet
- Protective gloves
- Tin snips
- File
- Blanket or carpet square
- Hammer
- Medium copper wire, 13 feet
- Bench vise
- Cup hook
- Drill and 1/8-inch bit

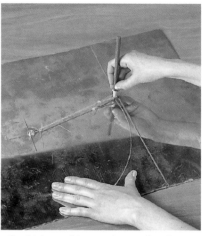

1 Using a china marker and a piece of looped string, mark a 17³/₄-inch circle on the 0.9 mm copper sheet.

2 Wearing protective gloves, cut out the circle with a pair of tin snips. Carefully smooth any sharp edges using a file.

3 Put the copper on a blanket and hammer it lightly from the center. Spread the pockets out to the rim. Repeat, starting from the center each time, for the desired shape.

4 To make the perch, loop some copper wire and hold the ends in a vise. Fasten a cup hook into the chuck of a hand drill or slow-speed power drill. Put the cup hook through the loop. Run the drill to twist the wire. Drill three 1/8-inch holes around the rim of the bath. Bend a knot into one end of three 1-yard lengths of wire. Thread the wires through the holes from beneath the bath. Slip the twisted wire over two of the straight wires to form a perch, and hang in a suitable position.

Miniature Dovecote

This charming miniature dovecote adds a formal note to a window box. It is best not left out in the rain, however, so you might prefer to house it permanently in an indoor conservatory.

TOOLS AND MATERIALS

- ¹/₄-inch-thick balsa wood
- Pencil
- Ruler
- Scalpel or craft knife
- White glue
- White acrylic paint
- Medium paintbrushes
- Gray sugar paper
- I foot (¹/₄ x ¹/₄-inch) balsa wood stick
- Wood stain

1 Mark the six-sided floors onto the balsa wood, following the template at the back of the book. Cut out using a scalpel or craft knife.

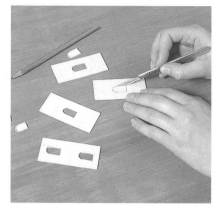

3 Cut the openings, making several light passes with the scalpel or craft knife rather than a single heavy cut. Cut out the perches.

2 Cut the wall panels, angling the long edge cuts so the pieces will fit together neatly.

4 Cut out the roof triangles and glue them together to form a cone. Paint all the parts and let dry. Assemble the house using glue. Cover the roof in sugar paper marked with pencil lines to resemble a tiled roof. Cut a stand from a stick of balsa wood colored with wood stain.

Dutch Dovecote

This sophisticated house has room for five pairs of occupants, all separated by internal dividing floors. The roof is removable, as are the internal floors, allowing for end-of-season cleaning.

TOOLS AND MATERIALS

- ½-inch medium-density fiberboard or exterior-grade plywood
- Pencil
- Ruler
- Saw
- Protractor
- Adjustable bevel
- Bench vise
- Plane
- Drill
- Keyhole saw
- White glue
- Wood scraps
- Air-dry modeling clay
- Rolling pin
- Table knife
- Cupboard doorknob wrapped in sheet metal or painted gray
- Latex paint: white and gray
- Medium paintbrushes
- Exterior-grade varnish

1 Mark the pieces of the dovecote onto fiberboard or plywood following the template provided. Cut out the pieces with a saw.

2 Use a protractor to set an 18-degree angle on an adjustable bevel.

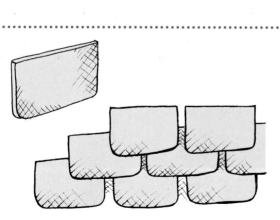

3 Hold the adjustable bevel against each of the ten wood strips and mark the 18-degree angle onto each end with a pencil line.

4 Join the pencil lines along the face of each strip. Carefully run the pencil down evenly along the edge. You may find it easier to use a ruler.

5 Position each strip in a vise and use a plane to remove the waste material down to the marked line. Repeat steps 3–5 for each of the ten roof triangles.

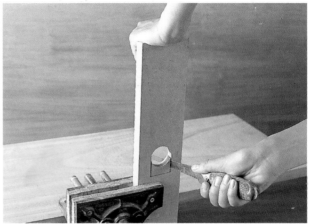

6 Cut ascending entrance holes in five of the ten wall strips, using a drill and a keyhole saw. Assemble the walls of the house, and glue together along the joints and to the circular base. Cut 6 small wooden blocks from wood scraps to use as supports for the removable floors. Attach three at even intervals one-third of the way up the inside of the dovecote, and the remaining three two-thirds of the way up. The dividing floors will simply rest on top of these. Glue the roof triangles to each other but not to the house, so the roof and floors are removable for cleaning. Roll out the modeling clay and cut into tile shapes, using the template as a guide. Glue to the roof base, adding the decorated doorknob at the apex as a finial. Paint the body of the house. Varnish the paint and the surface of the roof tiles so the decorative finish will withstand all weather conditions.

•••▶

In the nineteenth century, any self-respecting manor house would have had a full-size brick dovecote such as this. Sometimes used nowadays as residential buildings or studio workshops, their original function was to keep on hand a supply of fresh meat for cold winter months or an impromptu meal when guests arrived with short notice.

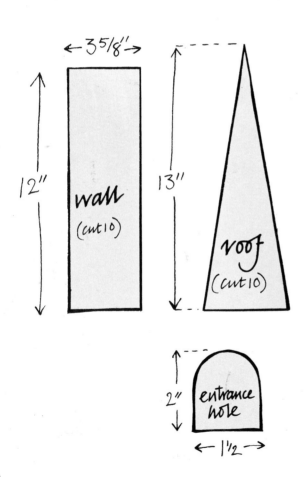

←— 3⅝″ —→

12″

wall
(cut 10)

13″

roof
(cut 10)

2″

entrance hole

←— 1½ —→

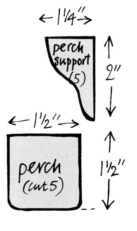

←— 1¼″ —→

perch support (5)

2″

←— 1½″ —→

perch (cut 5)

1½″

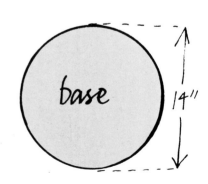

base

14″

Clapboard Meeting House

The birds who rear their brood in this New England-style house will be the envy of the neighborhood.

. . . .

TOOLS AND MATERIALS

- 1/4-inch medium-density fiberboard or plywood
- Pencil
- Ruler
- Saw
- White glue
- Hammer
- Paneling pins
- Birch veneer
- Colored woodstain
- Scalpel or craft knife
- 1/16 x 3/4-inch balsa wood strips
- Compass
- Latex paint: off-white, dark brown and brilliant white
- Medium and fine paintbrushes
- Exterior-grade varnish
- Drill with 1/8-inch bit
- 2 x 2-inch wooden post
- Screwdriver
- 3-inch screw, plus smaller screws

. . . .

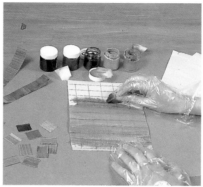

1 Mark the basic house onto fiberboard following the template at the back of the book. Cut out the pieces and assemble using white glue and paneling pins. Mark a sheet of veneer into 3/4 x 1 1/2-inch shingles and rub randomly with woodstain. Cut out the shingles with a scalpel or craft knife. Glue them in overlapping rows to the roof of the house.

2 Cut balsa wood strips to length to use as clapboarding. Glue in position. Set a compass as a scribe to transfer the cutting angles or make paper templates to indicate the shapes to be cut. Paint the clapboarding with off-white latex paint and the windows dark brown. Paint on window frames and doors using a fine artist's brush and white latex paint. Seal the house with exterior-grade varnish.

3 Cut an 8 x 5-inch base from fiberboard. Drill 1/8-inch pilot holes at each corner and in the center. Fasten to the top of the wooden post with a central 3-inch screw. Screw through the corner holes into the base of the house.

Folk-Art Titmouse Box

This perfect springtime retreat makes an extremely restful spot for hole nesters.

....

TOOLS AND MATERIALS

- $1/4$-inch medium-density fiberboard or exterior-grade plywood
- Small piece of rough-edged timber *(for base)*
- Pencil
- Ruler
- Saw
- Drill
- Keyhole saw
- White glue
- Hammer
- Paneling pins
- Latex paint: blue-gray and white
- Medium paintbrush
- Medium-grade sandpaper
- Lead sheet
- Tin snips
- Staple gun and staples
- Copper wire
- Wire cutters

....

1 Mark the basic house onto fiberboard following the template at the back of the book. Cut out the entrance hole as for the Beach Huts. Use white glue and paneling pins to assemble the basic house. Attach only the shorter roof piece. Paint the whole house, including the loose roof piece, with blue-gray latex paint. When dry, paint the walls of the house white. When dry (2–3 hours), distress by rubbing with medium-grade sandpaper until a small amount of the darker undercoat shows through randomly. Cut a strip of lead the depth of the roof by 2 inches and staple this to the loose roof half. Position the roof halves together, bend the lead to fit and staple through the lead into the attached roof half.

Right: The box can be adapted with different embellishments, and can be attached to a pole or hung from a tree, as here.

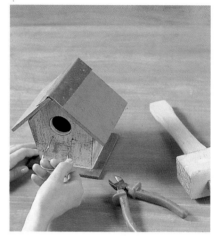

2 Drill two small holes just below and to either side of the entrance hole. Bend a piece of copper wire into a flattened loop slightly wider than the distance between the holes. Pass the two ends of the wire through the holes and turn them down $1/2$ inch inside the box to hold the perch in place.

Glass Gazebo Feeder

Constructed from recycled tin cans and small pieces of glass, this converted lantern will look like a jewel nestled in the leaves.

. . . .

TOOLS AND MATERIALS

- Glass lantern
- Tape measure (optional)
- Thin glass (optional)
- China marker (optional)
- T-square (optional)
- Glass cutter (optional)
- Ruler
- Protective gloves
- Shiny tin can (not aluminum), washed and dried
- Tin snips
- Flux and soldering iron
- Solder
- Fine wire mesh

. . . .

1 The lantern used here required extra glass to be installed. If this is the case, measure the areas required and reduce all measurements by 1/4 inch to allow for the metal border around each glass panel. Using a china marker, mark the reduced measurements on the glass, then cut out the pieces. Run a glass cutter in a single pass along a ruler, then tap along the score line. It is advisable to wear gloves.

2 Wearing protective gloves, and taking care to avoid injury on sharp edges, cut 3/8-inch strips of metal from a used tin can using tin snips. Wrap a strip of metal around each edge of each glass panel. Trim, then smear a small amount of soldering flux onto the adjoining surfaces of each corner.

3 Solder the corner joints of each panel. Heat up a joint using a soldering iron and apply solder until it flows between the surfaces to be joined. Remove the heat source. The solder will set after 1–2 seconds. Remember that the metal will remain hot for some time after the heat source is removed.

4 Measure the openings for the hoppers and fold sections of metal to fit, using a T-square or ruler to keep the fold lines straight. Solder the meeting points of each hopper. Cut out a platform from fine wire mesh and solder the platform, the panels and the hoppers in place on the gazebo framework.

Hansel and Gretel Cottage

The ultimate fairy-tale cottage, this two-story residence with its separate entrances and interior accommodation will brighten up the most somber garden vista, delighting visiting birds and children alike.

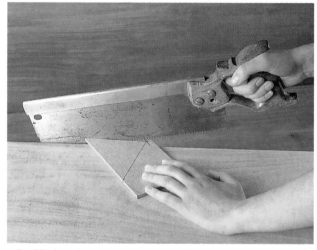

TOOLS AND MATERIALS

- ¹/₄-inch medium-density fiberboard or exterior-grade plywood
- Ruler
- T-square
- Pencil
- Saw
- Glue gun and glue sticks
- Scalpel or craft knife
- ¹/₄-inch balsa wood
- Latex paint: pink, blue, white, dark gray, terra-cotta, tile red and green
- Medium and fine paintbrushes
- Mounting board
- Drill
- Keyhole saw
- Acrylic or watercolor paints: various colors
- ¹/₁₆-inch balsa wood
- ¹/₁₆ x ¹/₈-inch balsa wood strips
- 4-inch hinge strip
- Screwdriver
- Screws
- Double-sided tape
- Scissors
- Fine sawdust
- Exterior-grade varnish

1 Mark and cut out the pieces of fiberboard following the template at the back of the book. Assemble pieces 1–8 in order by gluing them together. Cut a 'V' in the porch roof (piece 9) as marked on the template.

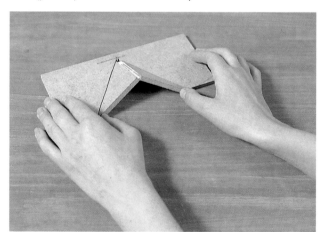

2 Glue the two roof triangle pieces into the 'V' of the porch roof and glue along the ridge.

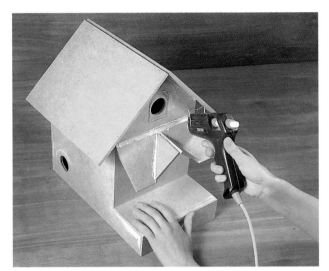

3 Glue the completed porch roof to the front of the house. Using a scalpel or craft knife, cut four $1/4$ x $1/4$-inch balsa wood posts, $4^1/4$ inches long, and glue them in place to support the porch roof. Make sure the posts are upright when viewed from the side as well as from the front. Paint the house with the pink, blue and white latex paints.

4 Mark and cut window and door frames from mounting board, following the templates. Use a window frame shape as a template to make shutters. Using first a drill and then a keyhole saw, cut entrance holes through the house wall where the top front window shape and side door will be. Hold each frame temporarily in position and draw around it with a soft pencil onto the wall. Paint the area within each drawn shape dark gray and let dry. Paint curtains onto the dark gray with acrylic or watercolor paints. When dry, glue the cut-out window and door frames in place. Decorate the shutter halves with appliqué hearts cut from $1/16$-inch-thick balsa and glue on each side of the window frames.

5 Measure from the house walls to the porch corner posts and from the corner posts to the porch center posts. Cut picket fence posts and top rails from $1/16$ x $1/8$-inch balsa wood and glue in place.

•••▶

6 Fit a small dividing wall of fiberboard between the main house area and underneath the veranda to prevent young birds from being trapped below.

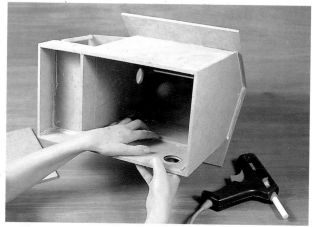

7 Glue a strip of fiberboard halfway up two of the interior walls. Cut the removable dividing floor from fiberboard and position it inside the house so that it is supported on the strips when the house is upright. Hinge the house to the base at the bottom of the rear wall, making it possible to raise the house and remove the interior dividing floor for cleaning. Cut out the gable and ridge decoration pieces from 1/16-inch balsa wood and glue each in place.

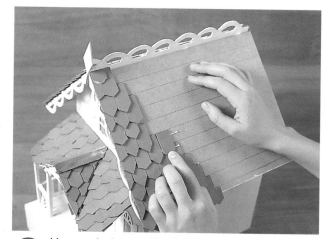

8 Use a scalpel to cut 3/4 x 1 1/2-inch roof tiles from mounting board, trimming one end of each tile to form a shallow V. Lay strips of double-sided tape on a work surface and press the tiles onto the tape. Paint over all the tiles in patches of various shades of terra-cotta and tile red. Let dry. Mark out the roof in horizontal lines 3/4 inch apart and begin tiling, lining up the head of each row of tiles with the penciled lines. Cut the first tile of each alternate row in half lengthwise so that the adjoining tiles will cover the seam of the tiles in the row below. Complete the painted decoration by touching in any terra-cotta missing at the roof tile edges and painting ivy and flowers on the sides of the house. Mix sawdust with green paint to give texture to the grassy areas. When all the decoration is dry, give the whole house several coats of weatherproof varnish to finish.

Lavender Hideaway

This hand-painted project takes only a short time to prepare using an inexpensive purchased birdhouse as the basic design. Even the heaviest shower rolls right off the lead roof, leaving the occupants warm and dry within. Take great care when cutting the lead, wearing protective gloves if at all possible.

TOOLS AND MATERIALS

- Wooden birdhouse
- Lilac latex paint
- Medium and fine paintbrushes
- Pencil
- Acrylic or watercolor paints: various colors
- Exterior-grade varnish
- Paper for pattern
- Scissors
- Protective gloves
- Thin sheet of lead
- Tin snips or craft knife
- Soft hammer or wooden mallet

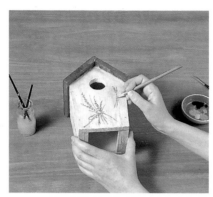

1 Paint the birdhouse with soft lilac latex paint and let dry. Sketch out the decorative design using a pencil. Fill in the sketch using acrylic or watercolor paints. When the paint is dry, cover the whole house with several coats of exterior-grade matte varnish.

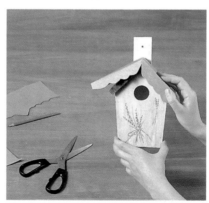

2 Make a paper pattern to fit the roof, using the template at the back of the book as a guide. Allow ¹/₂ inch extra for turning under each side and the rear, and 1¹/₄ inches extra for the scallops.

3 Transfer the design onto a thin sheet of lead and cut out using tin snips or a craft knife. Wash your hands thoroughly afterwards.

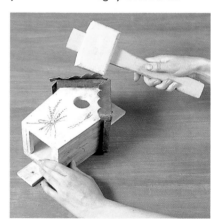

4 Hold the lead roof in place and mold into shape by tapping the lead with a soft hammer or wooden mallet until the correct fit is achieved. Turn the ¹/₂-inch allowance under at the back and at the eaves to secure the roof.

44

Log Cabin

This cabin is constructed around a basic box with a sloping roof. You can almost see a wisp of smoke curling from the chimney to welcome a tired bird home after a long day gathering food for hungry chicks.

TOOLS AND MATERIALS

- 1/4-inch medium-density fiberboard or exterior-grade plywood
- Ruler
- Pencil
- Saw
- Twigs and branches
- Axe or small-scale log splitter
- Glue gun and glue sticks
- Dark gray latex paint
- Medium paintbrush
- Drill
- Keyhole saw
- 4 x 1/2-inch coach bolt
- Moss or moss-covered branch

1 Mark the basic house onto fiberboard following the template at the back of the book. Cut out the pieces. Make logs from small branches by splitting the branches lengthwise, so there is a flat side for sticking to the box and a rounded surface with bark for the exterior face. Assemble the basic box with a glue gun and paint it with dark gray latex paint so any small gaps between the logs will not show when they are attached.

2 Glue the logs to the front of the house. Cut through the logs into the interior box using a drill and then a keyhole saw.

3 Cut a 1/2-inch hole and insert a coach bolt for the chimney. Continue to attach logs to the rest of the house, shaping them to fit and making the roof logs overlap the walls slightly as an added protection against rainfall. Neaten the corners of the walls by trimming the individual log ends with a saw. Glue a piece of moss or moss-covered branch to the opening as a perch.

Thatched Flint Cottage

The inspiration for this charming cottage comes from traditional thatched roofs.

....

TOOLS AND MATERIALS

- ¼-inch medium-density fiberboard or exterior-grade plywood
- Ruler
- Pencil
- Saw
- Glue gun and glue sticks
- Drill and ¼-inch bit
- Keyhole saw
- Double-sided tape
- Exterior-grade filler
- Small round pebble-like shingles
- Wheat straw
- Thin, malleable wire
- Scalpel or craft knife
- Fine chicken wire
- Latex paint: light gray, dark gray and burgundy
- Medium and fine paintbrushes
- ⅛-inch balsa wood
- Exterior-grade varnish

....

1 Mark and cut out the basic house shapes from fiberboard, following the template at the back of the book, and glue the shapes together. Cut an entrance hole, using the drill and keyhole saw. Cut out window and door shapes from fiberboard and temporarily hold them in place with double-sided tape.

2 Apply a thick layer of exterior-grade filler to a small area of the outside of the house. Press shingles into the surface of the filler. Continue to apply filler and to press in shingle until the whole house is covered, except for the window and door shapes. Gently remove the temporary window and door masks and set aside for use as templates.

3 Gather together bundles of about 25 wheat straws and tie with thin wire. Glue tied bundles onto the roof of the house until the whole roof is covered. Trim the thatch at the eaves with a scalpel or craft knife and wrap the completed roof with fine chicken wire to secure the thatch.

4 Paint the door and window openings light gray. Paint a lattice of dark gray over the light gray to resemble leaded-light windows. Draw around the window templates onto thin balsa wood and cut out window frames and sills to fit. Make a door from balsa wood and paint it burgundy. Glue the door and window pieces in place. Paint the base dark gray and coat all exposed wood and paintwork with several layers of varnish.

Rapunzel's Tower

Hidden away in the forest, this romantic tower is truly exclusive. Because it is made from found objects, the look is dependent on the available materials.

. . . .

TOOLS AND MATERIALS

- Paper for template
- Pencil
- Garden twine
- Ruler
- Scissors
- 6-inch diameter tubing
- 0.9 mm copper sheet, 18 x 18 inches
- China marker
- Protective gloves
- Tin snips
- File
- Drill and 1/8-inch bit and 1/4-inch cutter bit
- Rivet tool and 1/8-inch rivets
- Glue gun and glue sticks
- 0.2 mm copper foil, 1 x 2 inches
- 2 1/2-inch nail or wire
- Twigs

. . . .

1 Make a paper pattern for the cone-shaped roof to fit around the tubing; add a 3/4-inch overlap for joining the edges. Transfer the pattern onto a piece of thin copper sheet with a china marker. Wearing protective gloves, cut out the shape using tin snips. File off any sharp edges or snags. Bend the copper into a cone shape with an overlap and check that it fits the tubing correctly. Adjust this if necessary.

2 Drill 1/8-inch holes at intervals through both layers of copper along the overlap and fasten the overlap using blind rivets. Squeeze the handle of the rivet gun until the rivet shaft snaps off, securing the overlap firmly. Glue the cone in place on top of the tubing.

3 Make a flag for the rooftop by cutting a wavy flag shape from copper foil. Cut a sideways 'V' in one end of the flag and bend the other end around a nail or short piece of wire as a flagpole. Glue in place at the tip of the roof.

4 Make a rope ladder by passing cut lengths of small twigs through the weave of two lengths of twine. Cut an entrance hole with tin snips and glue the ladder in place.

Palladian Bird Table

This classical-style feeding table, whether pole-, tree- or wall-mounted, is easy to make and will beautify any setting.

● ●

TOOLS AND MATERIALS

- 1/2-inch medium-density fiberboard or exterior-grade plywood *(for the base)*
- 1/4-inch medium-density fiberboard or exterior-grade plywood
- Ruler
- Pencil
- Saw
- Glue gun and glue sticks
- 8 threaded knobs, 1 1/4 inches diameter x 3/4 inches deep
- 4 dowels, 4 3/4 x 5/8 inches
- Drill and 1/8-inch bit
- Exterior-grade filler
- Fine-grade sandpaper
- Medium paintbrush
- Off-white latex paint
- Exterior-grade varnish

● ●

1 Mark and cut out all the pieces, following the template at the back of the book. Assemble the base and steps with hot glue. Mark the positions of the columns at each corner of the top step and on the underside of the ceiling.

2 Glue the main gable triangles onto each end of the ceiling piece.

●●●▶

3 Glue each half of the roof onto the top of the gable triangles. Make sure each roof half overlaps the ceiling by the same amount at the sides and each end.

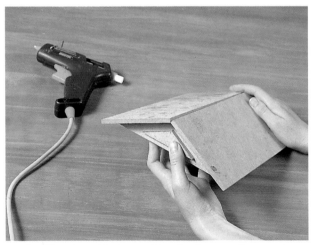

4 Glue the gable decorative triangle centrally onto the face of the front gable.

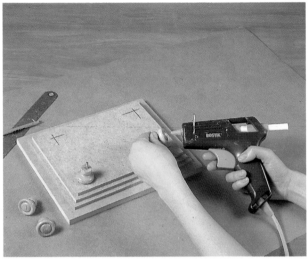

5 Glue the threaded cupboard knobs in position at each corner mark on the base and the ceiling.

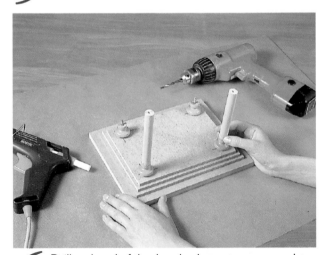

6 Drill each end of the dowel columns to accommodate the protruding thread of the knobs. Apply glue to each thread and assemble the dowels between the base and the roof. Fill any gaps with exterior-grade filler, rub down with fine-grade sandpaper and paint with off-white emulsion followed by several coats of exterior-grade varnish.

Templates

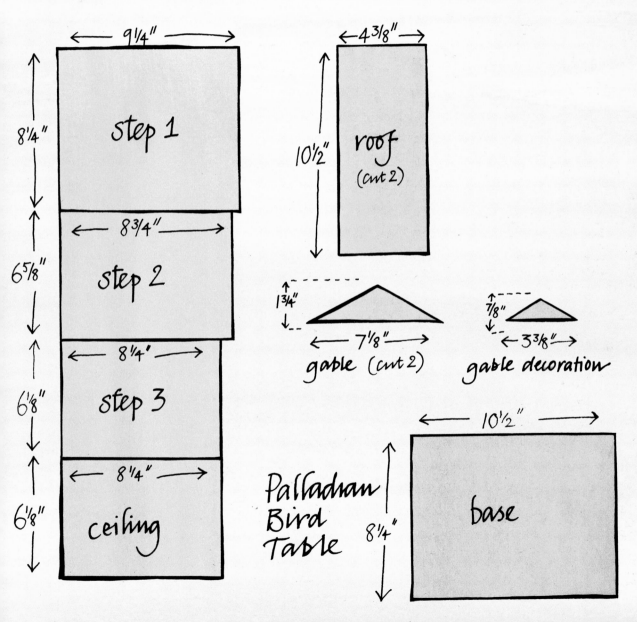

9¼"

8¼"

step 1

6⅝"

8¾"

step 2

6⅛"

8¼'

step 3

6⅛"

8¼"

ceiling

4⅜"

10½"

roof

(cut 2)

1¾"

7⅛"

gable (cut 2)

⅞"

3⅜"

gable decoration

Palladian
Bird
Table

10½"

base

8¼"

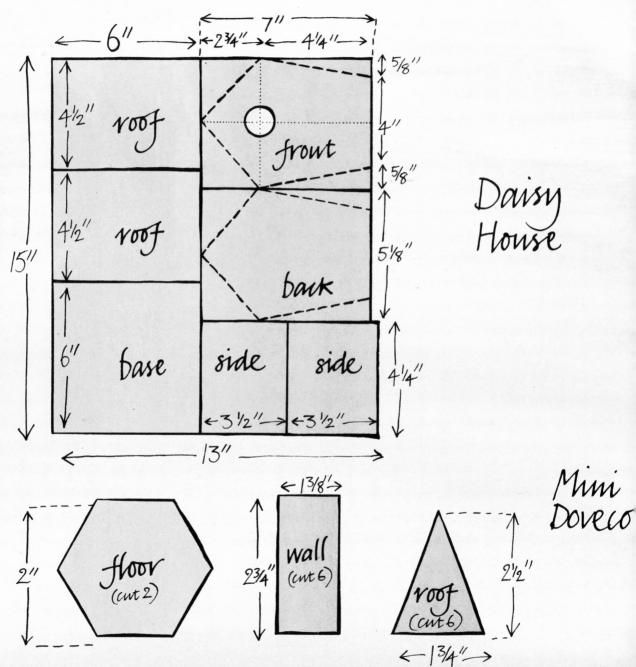

Daisy
House

Mini
Doveco

Beach Huts

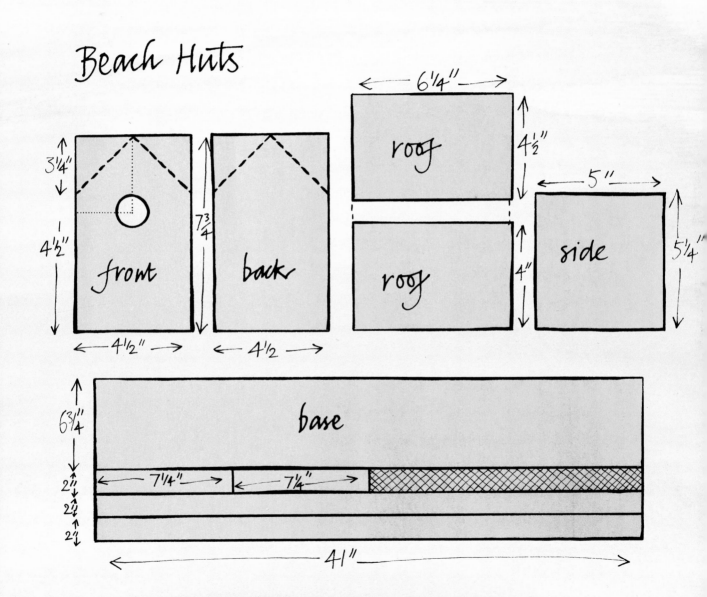

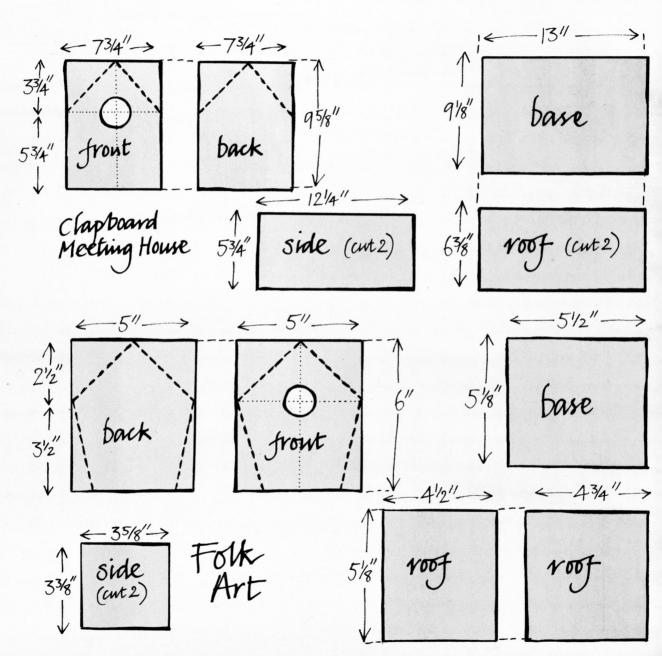

7¾"

3¾"

5¾"

front

7¾"

9⅝"

back

Clapboard
Meeting House

12¼"

5¾" side (cut 2)

13"

9⅛" base

6⅜" roof (cut 2)

5"

2½"

3½" back

5"

6

front

5½"

5⅛" base

3⅝"

3⅜" side
(cut 2)

Folk
Art

4½"

5⅛" roof

4¾"

roof

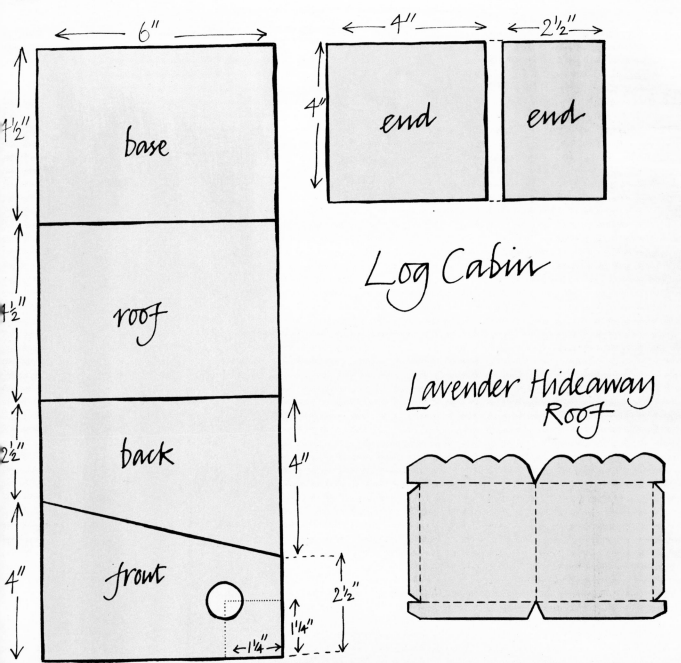

6"

1½"

base

4½"

roof

2½"

back

4"

front

4"

2½"

1¼"

1¼"

4"

4"

2½"

end

2½"

end

Log Cabin

Lavender Hideaway
Roof

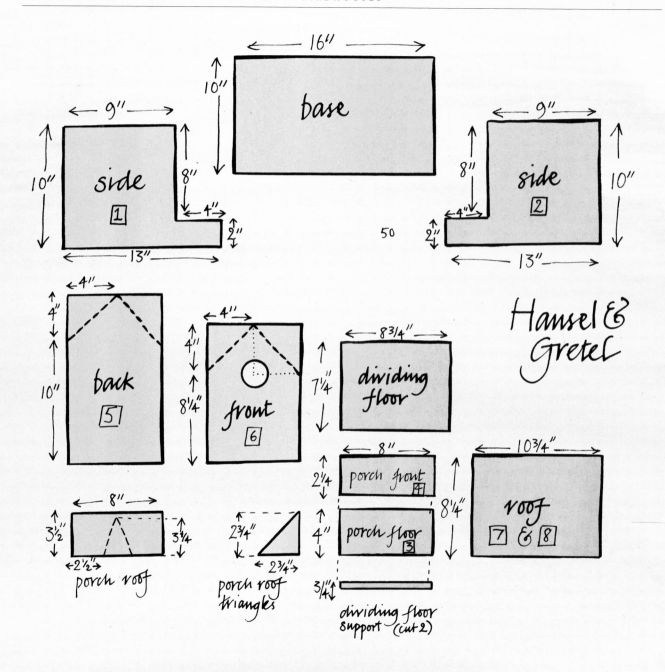

16"

base

10"

9"

side
1

10"

8"

4"

2"

13"

9"

side
2

8"

4"

2"

10"

13"

50

Hansel &
Gretel

4"

4"

back
5

10"

4"

4"

front
6

8¼"

8¾"

dividing
floor

7¼"

8"

porch front
4

2¼"

10¾"

roof
7 & 8

8¼"

8"

porch roof

3½"

3¾"

2½"

porch floor
3

4"

2¾"

porch roof
triangles

2¾"

¾"

dividing floor
support (cut 2)

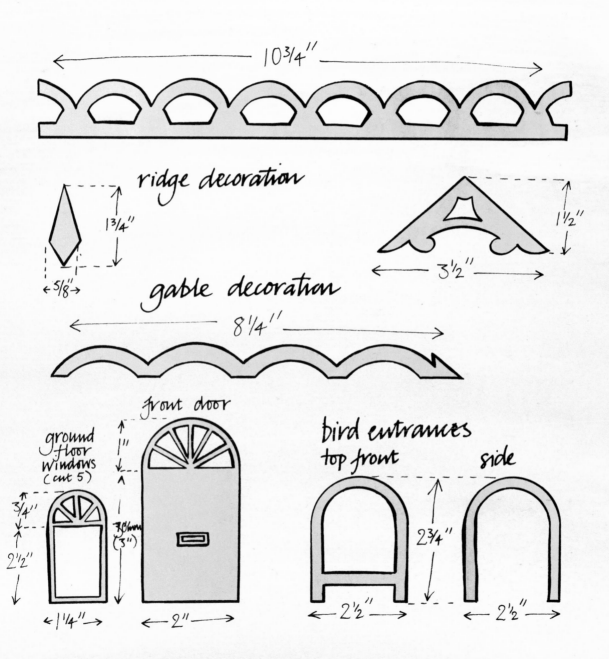

10¾″

ridge decoration

1¾″   5/8″

gable decoration

1½″   3½″

8¼″

front door

ground floor windows (cut 5)

bird entrances
top front   side

1″

¾″

2½″

76mm (3″)

1¼″   2″

2¾″

2½″   2½″

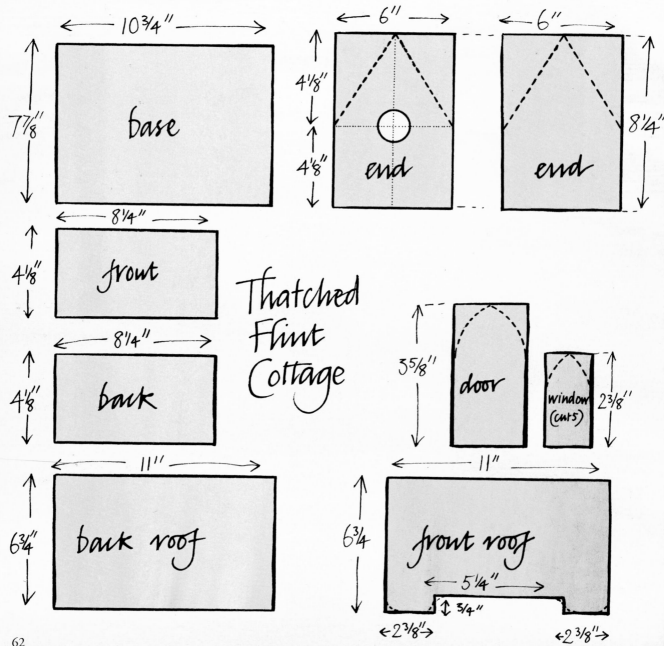

10¾"

base

7⅞"

6"

4⅛"

4⅛"

end

6"

8¼"

end

8¼"

front

4⅛"

8¼"

back

4⅛"

Thatched
Flint
Cottage

3⅝"

door

window
(cut 5)

2⅜"

11"

back roof

6¾"

11"

front roof

6¾

5¼"

¾"

2⅜"

2⅜"

Additional Information

WILDLIFE ORGANIZATIONS

National Audubon Society
700 Broadway
New York, NY 10003
(212) 979-3000

American Birding Association
P.O. Box 6599
Colorado Springs, CO 80934

American Ornithologists' Union
National Museum of Natural History
Smithsonian Institute
Washington, DC 20560

Bird Feeders Society
P.O. Box 225
Mystic, CT 06355

National Wildlife Federation
(Backyard Wildlife Habitat Program)
1400 Sixteenth Street, NW
Washington, DC 20036-2266

Sierra Club
730 Polk Street
San Francisco, CA 94109

World Wildlife Fund
1250 Twenty-fourth Street, NW,
Suite 200
Washington, DC 20037

Bird Watcher's Digest
P.O. Box 110
Marietta, OH 45750-0110

Birder's World
720 East 8th Street
Holland, MI 49423

ADDITIONAL READING

Birdscaping Your Garden, George Adams, Rodale Press, 1994

The Birdfeeder Book, Donald and Lillian Stokes, Little, Brown and Co., 1987

The Backyard Birdwatcher, George Harrison, Fireside, 1983

Birdhouses, Peri Wolfman and Charles Gold, Clarkson Potter, 1993

The Garden Bird Book, edited by David Glue, Macmillan, 1982

PICTURE CREDITS

Michelle Garrett: p. 11 bottom; Habitat: p. 8 top; Debbie Patterson: p. 14, p. 15 (Designer: Cleo Mussi); Spike Powell: p. 2; Wildbird Foods Ltd.: p. 11 top left and top right.

AUTHORS' ACKNOWLEDGMENTS

We would like to thank the following people who contributed so much to this project in terms of support, advice and locations for photography:

Dominique Coughlin, for putting us in touch with Carlo Jolly, who supplied the Beach Huts.
Dave Chitson, of Stilmore Homes, for the Miniature Dovecote.
Forsham Cottage Arks for the loan of the wall-mounted dovecote, shelf and terra-cotta feeders and pots.

Thanks to Bostik for supplying glues and glue guns; 3M for spray adhesives; Crown Paints for paint products and Bosch for power tools.

Thanks to Chris and Pat Cutforth for their stunning locations and ornithological advice, and Robin Nelson for additional advice on birds.

Thanks to the National Trust for permitting photography at Avebury Manor, and to Dr and Mrs Cameron for permission to photograph their barn and dovecote.

Index

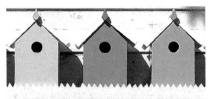